THE LINEAGE
Breaking The Cycle

Julie Wigfall

Copyright © 2020 by Julie Wigfall
The Lineage: Breaking The Cycle
Breakingdacycle@gmail.com

All rights reserved. No part of this book may be used or reproduced by any means, graphic, electronic, or mechanical, including photocopying, recording, taping or by any information storage retrieval system,without the written permission of the publisher except in the case of brief quotations embodied in critical articles and reviews.

Entegrity Choice Publishing
PO Box 453
Powder Springs, GA 30127

Designed by: Woznica Book Design
woznicabookdesign@gmail.com

The views expressed in this work are solely those of the author and do not reflect the views of the publisher, and the publisherhereby disclaims any responsibility for them.

Names used in this publication have been changed to protect the privacy of the individuals.

Library of Congress Cataloging-in-Publication Data
ISBN: 978-1-7325767-9-7
Library of Congress Control Number: 2019909303

ACKNOWLEDGMENTS

First, I want to give honor to God, Who is the Head of my life. God, You receive all the praise and glory. Thank You for using this empty vessel to tell a story, to break chains of bondage, and to change lives.

I want to thank a young woman by the name of Ashley Hicks. She awakened my dream to write this book, my story which lay dormant inside of me. Meeting a published author who had written her own story, stirred something deep inside of me to take action. I would also like to thank Erica Jackson, Daryl Patterson, and Kamika Winfrey for their support and encouragement.

Contents

Acknowledgments iii
Introduction vii

Chapter 1
A Glimpse Into the Past 1

Chapter 2
The Boogeyman: The Cycle Is Introduced .. 3

Chapter 3
Why Me? 7

Chapter 4
Invisible 11

Chapter 5
Day of Sorrow 15

Chapter 6
The Seed of the Cycle Is Planted 23

Chapter 7
Black (The Snake): Same Script—
Different Cast 33

Chapter 8
Reggie Mack Jr. 37

Chapter 9
The Meet and Greet 41

Chapter 10
Let's Play House 45

Chapter 11
Web of Deceit 51

Chapter 12
   Flag on the Play 57
Chapter 13
   Almost Doesn't Count 63
Chapter 14
   The Dream that Died 67
Chapter 15
   Something to Live For 71
Chapter 16
   When Hope Fail 77
Chapter 17
   The Pain Of Fatherhood 81
Chapter 18
   Hey, Death, Come and Get Me 85
Epilogue 87

Introduction

This book was written from a personal account of the effects of generational cycles of sexual, emotional, and psychological abuse and addiction within my family. My own experiences inspired me to share my story in hopes of breaking or helping to break these cycles in other families. After being a victim, I found deliverance from emotional scars, drug addiction, verbal abuse, and psychological triggers—mostly formed by my parents, Margaret and Reggie.

My parents were victims of unhealed and unaddressed abuse. Sadly, my parents never received the help they needed to heal from their emotional scars. They grew into the lifestyles they had learned, continued the same behaviors, and inhabited the same environments that enabled the cycle to continue. They abused drugs to numb themselves and cope with the pains of reality they faced daily, until the ultimate end.

The lifeline of hope that broke the bondage of generational oppression for me began with inviting Jesus Christ into my life. God loves us and wants to set us free from anything that cripples our lives. It is my sincere hope that this book releases a cycle-breaking anointing over the cycle of generational curses in your life.

I pray that your story changes today! You can start living your best life as you welcome the freedom that comes with deliverance through Jesus Christ.

1

A Glimpse Into the Past
Margaret

I felt like dying as I sat on the cold floor trying to comfort myself. I was in an abandoned building, which echoed loneliness, rocking back and forth to shake off the cold chill as the warmth of my tears ironically trickled down my face. One of the lyrics in Edgar Winter's "Dying to Live", calmed my mind as I sat waiting for death. "Why am I dying to live, if I'm just living to die?"

Life had been no walk in the park for me. I thought the only solution to escape my pain was death. I looked around the room at others—some asleep, a few zoned out—and I took a deep breath. I couldn't help but inhale the stale smell of urine and burnt plastic before my breath released.

Chuckling to myself, I thought, "Hmph, this must be the fragrance of the day, my perfume."

With my arms wrapped tightly around myself, I began rocking back and forth again, as painful memories played on the screen of my mind. I imagined I was looking at a movie starring Me.

2

THE BOOGEYMAN: THE CYCLE IS INTRODUCED

Margaret

I remember a day when I was sitting in class listening to a conversation among fellow classmates. One conversation I heard puzzled me deeply. They were discussing people and scary icons they feared the most such as Frankenstein, Zombie, Dracula, etc. I was puzzled because I had no clue at that moment whom I feared. I had yet to encounter the most-feared individual in my life, but had it been a couple of years later, I'm not sure if I would have been honest or hesitant about the monster who scared the life out of me. No nightmare and no character from a horror movie would ever compare to Melvin, my stepdad. He was a real live monster.

I can recall horrendous nights of abuse vividly, almost as if it were just yesterday. I remember the routine so intensely. There I would be, lying in the dark, in total silence. I would immediately stop breathing when I heard the creaking sound of the door opening. Knowing exactly what was coming next, one might think I should have been used to it. After all, it was his daily routine. Melvin violated me daily. This man, my stepdad, had been raping me for several years, nevertheless, it was impossible to get used to such violation.

As he climbed on top of me, I thought I felt my spirit leave my body. I felt as if I was watching myself from the corner of the room — an out of body experience. I watched sweat pour from his forehead as he stared at me. The smell of gin, his favorite cologne, and the grunts he whispered in my ear to signal how good it was, made my whole being cringe. I watched myself lying there motionless, wanting to die. I wanted to cry. I wanted to save myself, but I didn't know how.

As my spirit came back into my body, I disconnected my mind from my body and traveled to another location with another family in another time. God knows I wanted to be anywhere but here, and far, far, away from enduring another rape. The next morning as I prepared for school, I stopped and took a good look at myself in the mirror. I had no clue who the person looking back at me was. I did not recognize my own reflection. I saw a girl fading into a dark abyss, piece by piece. My stepdad was draining my soul, and I had no way to stop him.

3

WHY ME?
Margaret

As I stared at my face in the mirror, I was startled to see how deep my cheeks had sunken. There were dark circles under and around my eyes. Considering the condition of my face, I believed that the scars would be permanent, because each night, I cried myself to sleep. My mental state had taken its toll on my face. Moreover, it was clear my mental state had taken over my higher being. When I combed my hair, I was further taken aback. Running my fingers through my hair as I combed it, I realized that I had more hair between my fingers and in the sink than on my head.

I continued to examine myself in the mirror, questioning in my mind, "Why is this happening to me?" It became a repetitive conversation in my mind, "What did I do to deserve to be treated this way?" The pain of what I saw in the mirror made me cry out, "Lord, why is this happening to me?" Over and over again I asked God, "Why are you allowing me to live through this nightmare?"

Relentlessly, I asked God, "Why don't you save me?" Every time I was raped, I wanted to scream at the top of my lungs, but I would immediately resign not to do so. I felt my silent prayers bouncing back in my face, pushing me farther into the same dark hole. I decided not to scream, because I believed it wouldn't make any difference, and I also knew that it would be over soon. Truthfully, I had been screaming for a long time, but no one heard me. No one came to rescue me. Burying my pain was reality, not an option.

Time passed as I continued to stare at myself in the mirror, and I realized I needed to get a move on. I paused once more to analyze my appearance and finish getting dressed for school. I was preparing for school, but I really wanted to crawl back into bed and shut out the world. To make matters more complex, I had two exams awaiting me at school, which I was hardly prepared to take. It's hard to study when your thoughts revolve around sexual abuse instead of school.

Sifting through a pile of dirty clothes, I picked up several pieces to sniff in an effort to find an outfit presentable for school. That meant not looking like funky laundry or smelling like dirty clothes. Once I made my selection from the pile of dirty clothes on the floor, I polished my look off with my favorite Friday jeans and Reebok classic sneakers with holes in the soles. No big deal. I had been rocking those bad boys for the past two years.

I finally brushed my hair into a ponytail, grabbed my book bag and my house key, and headed out the door. Just as I reached the door, I realized I didn't have my music. My music was a must-have if I was going to attempt to make it through an insane day. I ran back to retrieve my music, before heading to school.

4

Invisible
Margaret

As I stepped outside, I inhaled deep breaths of cool air while taking note of the beauty around me and listening to the birds chirp. The cool air awakened my senses as the trees greeted me with a wave.

I love springtime in Augusta, Georgia. The weather is not too hot and not too cold, but just right. I plugged in my headphones and bobbed down the street towards the bus stop, with "Let's Go Crazy" by Prince blasting in my ears.

As I neared the bus stop where other kids were waiting, I kept my distance from them. The other kids seemed to be so happy. They had fresh clothes and shared a bond that I had yet to experience. In many ways, I envied them. I wished that I had just one person I could call a friend. As the bus approached, the crowd converted into a single line to get onto the bus. I walked slowly toward the bus, trying to make sure I was the last person to get on.

Unexpectedly, out of nowhere, some girl bumped into me as if I was invisible. She shouted, "Watch where you're going!" She looked me up and down like it was my fault that she was not watching where she was going. My knee-jerk reaction was to attack, but then I decided not to.

I usually sat close to the front of the bus, because the popular kids always headed to the back of the bus, which was their domain. I leaned back in the seat, with my headphones plugged in, eyes closed, and allowed my mind to get lost in the music. When I felt the bus slowing down to enter the side gate of the school, my palms and forehead began to sweat. My nerves were on edge as I thought to myself, "Can I get a break? Is there somewhere I can go and find peace?"

Between being verbally abused at school, and being verbally, sexually, and physically abused at home, I had no peace. I felt like I was being driven insane. I stayed seated while everyone got off the bus. I contemplated whether or not I was going to eat breakfast, because, lately, my appetite had increased.

When I got off the bus I observed the historic, red brick school building with its big white letters that read, "Lucy C. Laney." Lucy Craft Laney was an early African-American educator who in 1883 founded the first school for black children in Augusta, Georgia. Lucy Laney was selected by Governor Jimmy Carter in 1974 to be one of the first African Americans to have their portraits hung in the Georgia State Capitol.

You would think I would be proud and honored to be attending such a trail-blazing school, but instead, I took a deep breath wishing I was done with high school. As I entered the building, I walked toward the cafeteria. I quickly scanned the lines to see which one was the shortest, and pushed myself toward it, moving strategically and quietly. I selected milk, cereal, graham crackers, peaches, and orange juice to complete my meal. I found a table, isolated of course, and surreptitiously ate breakfast.

I chose to be isolated from the other kids at school. It seemed no matter how hard I tried to fit in at school, it never worked. Pretending to be someone I'm not, made me sick to my stomach, so I decided to be alone. The rolling trash barrel was in the center of the cafeteria, so I threw away my trash and continued outside to get lost in my music while I waited for the bell to ring. I had hoped it would be delayed, but as usual, the bell rang on time, and I had to get to class.

The day dragged on. I drifted from class to class, moving through the crowded hallways as I watched other kids pair off into groups. Seventh period, Mr. Henry's World History Class, finally started. Sitting there and trying to focus my mind was a challenge. I spent the entire period running through the maze of my mind, searching for an exit sign. Every single minute that passed, I wished that school was over, while at the same time dreading to go home. Just the thought of these two things made me sick.

5

Day of Sorrow
Margaret

Sitting at my desk, unprepared for the test Mr. Henry was passing out, I began to get sicker. I raised my hand.
"Yes, Margaret?" said Mr. Henry.
"Can I please be excused to the restroom?"
Looking at me over his glasses, Mr. Henry said, "You have five minutes before the test begins."
I rushed to the bathroom and instantly became hot, hurling into the toilet. I stood up so quickly that I became light-headed and slid down to the floor. I was trying to push everything out of my system, hoping it would make me feel better. I was eager for whatever it was to go away very soon. I stood up again and made my way to the sink to wash my hands. As I glared into the mirror, I hated the person looking back at me. I headed back to class to finish the rest of the school day.

When I got off the bus that afternoon, the sun welcomed me with its bright rays. Walking home, I felt sick. My head hurt, my stomach ached, and I felt the urge to throw up. I told myself that I needed to pick up the pace, but my body was not responding to what my mind commanded. I wondered if it could have been the shepherd's pie I ate for lunch. Oddly, something told me not to eat it.

I unlocked the front door and leaned against it as it opened. I took a deep breath and thanked God that there was no one home. Making my way to the kitchen, I poured a glass of water. I headed to the bathroom, grabbing the Pepto Bismol from the medicine cabinet. I downed a capful, although I hated it. It tasted like minty chalk, but I felt so bad I was open to trying anything, even if it didn't taste good. I opened the door to my room, dropped my book bag on the floor, took off my shoes, and crawled into bed. I made a promise to myself to get up and do my homework later.

Someone was yelling, "Margaret! Margaret!" It startled me out of my sleep. I squinted through my tired eyes. As I woke up, I realized Mom was calling my name. I was too weak to say anything. I was sweating profusely.

"Girl, what's wrong with you?" she hollered.

I replied, "I've been feeling sick since lunch, and it's getting worse. I threw up after eating. I was hoping that after my lunch came back up I would feel better."

"What did you eat for lunch?" Mom asked.

"Shepherd's pie," I replied.

She blurted out, "Maybe you should take some Pepto Bismol?"

I told her that I'd taken some as soon as I got home but felt worst by the minute. Mama was a nurse at the University Hospital.

Struggling to get out of bed, I sat upright and threw up right next to Mom's feet.

"Child, get up and clean up this mess," Mom yelled in disgust. She shook her head and said, "I guess I will have to take you to the emergency room, even though I just got home."

I hung my head low as I mumbled to myself, "This is not my fault."

It seemed to me that all of my life, I had been fighting for my mom's love and attention. I didn't know why she didn't like me. As I tried to muster up enough energy to get moving, I stood up and saw specs of light, and then my world went black.

Unaware of what was happening around me, I awakened, cold and enclosed in bed rails. There was the constant beep of a monitor, and I could feel a cold solution running through my veins. I looked around the room and spotted Mom in a chair in the corner across the room. We made eye contact, but she didn't say one word. Just as

I was about to call out to her, the door swung open, and the doctor walked in.

The doctor said, "Hello Margaret, how are you feeling?"

"Better," I replied.

I glanced at Mom as the doctor approached me. I saw pure hatred in her eyes. This made me very uncomfortable, so I shifted my eyes back to the doctor.

He cleared his throat and said, "So Margaret, how long have you been feeling this way?"

"Just today," I replied.

He asked, "Do you know what caused you to be sick?"

"No," I replied.

I was becoming irritated by the questions. The doctor proceeded to say, "Margaret, are you aware that you are sixteen weeks pregnant?"

A lump formed in my throat as tears flowed down my face. The doctor was trying to calm me down, but I felt like I couldn't breathe. I kept saying, "No," over and over again, until eventually, the doctor gave me something to calm me down.

After I finally calmed down, I stared blankly at the wall. I heard Mom suck her teeth, then suddenly blurt out, "You are nothing but a ho!" Tears streamed down my face.

Mom continued asking questions:

"Guess you smellin' yourself, huh?"

"You think you are grown, huh?"

"What are you doing, embarrassing me at my place of work?"

"Who is this nappy-headed boy that got you pregnant?

"What's his name?"

I was silent. I didn't know what to say as I endured a verbal beat-down from my mom.

"Girl, you better answer me right now!" she shouted.

"Melvin," I blurted out.

As I said his name, it felt like the releasing of one thousand doves.

"Where do this Melvin stay?" she asked.

"With us," I said.

Mom froze in place, not taking another step.

Startled, she asked, "Are you talking about my Melvin?"

I was just about to answer her, but the nurse walked into the room with discharge papers and told us that we were free to leave. We walked in silence to the car. I have never seen my mom walk so fast in her life.

When we arrived home, as we made our way up the steps into the house, I was moving fast toward my room when Mom screamed, "You stop right there!" By the tone of her voice, I knew she meant business.

"Melvin!" Mom yelled in an angry voice.

Just as Mom was about to continue going off on me, Melvin walked in from the kitchen with a beer in his hand.

"Hey babe," said Melvin, as he approached mom.

He tried to give her a kiss, but she pushed him away before his lips could touch hers.

"Baby, what's wrong?" he asked.

Mom said, "Have you been sleeping with my daughter?"

Melvin could have won the Best Actor award. He stood looking at her as if he was deeply hurt by the question. He seemed baffled that she would dare ask him such a question.

Eventually, he said, "Margaret is like a daughter to me. How can you ask me something like that?"

"I took Margaret to the doctor, and she is pregnant. She told me that you are the daddy." Mom said as she stood flat-footed with her arms folded demanding an explanation.

Melvin shouted, "You believe her over your husband? You said yourself that she is nothing but a liar."

Mom turned to me, and I yelled, "I am not lying!"

Before she could say a word, I blurted out, "He took the lock off my door, so I can no longer lock it to keep him out."

Mom looked surprised to hear that Melvin had done that. She asked Melvin, "Why did you take the lock off of her door?"

"I am not going back and forth with you and this liar. I told you that I didn't do it," he said calmly as he turned around in circles. He set the beer in his hand down and looked directly at my mom and said, "I don't have to take this. I'm going to pack my things."

Mom ran after him as he stormed down the hallway. Mom yelled, "Wait! Wait a minute!"

I turned and headed toward my room. When I reached my bed, I crawled in and cried myself to sleep. In the middle of the night, I was awakened by the two of them moaning and groaning from sex. I burst into tears knowing, at that point, that she wanted him no matter what he did.

Deep down inside, I believed Mom knew that I was telling the truth. Even a blind man could see the clues. I resigned myself to the belief that she just didn't care. I sat in bed, knees pulled up to my chest, softly repeating, "Why don't she love me?" as I rocked myself back and forth.

6

THE SEED OF THE CYCLE IS PLANTED
Margaret

The fury of the sun's bright rays bursting through the blinds awakened me. Sitting straight up in bed, I quickly realized there was someone in my room. I looked across the room and saw Mom moving around. She was grabbing my belongings and stuffing them into a suitcase. I called out to her, but she didn't respond. It appeared that she was in a daze.

Tears streamed down my face like a river. I was terrified, not able to figure out what would happen next. Finally, she stopped, looked at me, and shouted, "You have got to leave my house!"

"Mom, where am I going to go?" I shrieked.

She replied, "I don't know. Maybe you need to find the little nappy-headed boy that you laid up with. See if you can stay with him."

"I'm not lying, Mom!" I cried.

Before I could finish, she shouted, "Shut up girl!"

Mom shouted, "I will not let you lie about my husband or break up our home! I have to work tonight, and Melvin gets off at 4:00 P.M. I will allow you to take a bath and eat something, but you and your stuff need to be out of here before Melvin comes home."

Mom showed no emotion — only disdain. She turned her back toward me, grabbed her purse, and headed for the door, slamming it behind her. I was perplexed, bewildered, angry, and alone. I asked God,

"Why?" as I rocked backward and forward like a rocking chair.

I sat feeling numb in bed, thinking, "What did I do to deserve this?" At that very moment, I decided to stop talking to God. It was obvious, He didn't care. I remember saying to myself, "I don't love or trust anyone, and I never will." It seemed as if I had sat motionless in the same spot for hours. It was around 8:00 A.M when Mom told me I had to leave her house. Now, it was almost 1:00 P.M.

My entire being was cloaked in a cloud of dread as time ticked away. Fear obsessed me as I had no power to stop or slow time. I was scared. In just a few hours, I would be a homeless teenager. I knew I needed to get moving, so I took a

THE SEED OF THE CYCLE IS PLANTED

deep breath and jumped out of bed. I grabbed some clothes on my way to the bathroom. I wanted to enjoy a hot shower because I didn't know when I would get another one.

After I got dressed, I went into the kitchen and warmed up some leftovers. I sat for about thirty minutes devouring everything on my plate. I needed that free meal. When I finished eating, I grabbed my bag and pretty much went grocery shopping in Mom's kitchen, putting anything I could find in my sack. I only had a couple of dollars and knew it would not get me very far.

I went back into what used to be my room and noticed the clock which read 3:15 P.M. My heart pounded as my eyes began to fill with tears. Tears flowed like an open faucet as I looked around, saying softly to myself, "I have nowhere to go. I have nowhere to go."

Picking up my suitcase, sack of food, and CD player, I walked slowly toward the door. At the front door, I took a final long look at the place I had called home. As I closed the door behind me, I confessed, "I will never walk through these doors of hell again." It was final. I closed the door to the devil's house for the last time.

I had no idea where to go. I just picked a direction and started walking. There was no one I could call for help. As I walked, I tried to figure out what to do. My feet were moving, but I did not know where I was going. I remember being glad it was spring because it was neither too hot nor too cold.

After walking for quite some time, my feet began to ache. I was growing tired. I came upon a bus stop and decided to sit down to take a rest. Twenty minutes into my rest, a woman came and sat down on the opposite end of the bench. I simply sat there staring ahead. From the corner of my eye, I could see her looking at me. Finally, I looked her way and we made eye contact.

She spoke first, saying, "Hi, my name is Monica."

I said, "Hey, I'm Margaret."

"You must be going on a trip?" she asked.

"No, not really," I replied.

"Sorry, didn't mean to pry," she said.

After observing Monica, she seemed okay, so I blurted out, "I'm trying to find somewhere to go. I'm pregnant! My mom kicked me out of the house!"

It was comforting to observe her smile turn upside down. She appeared genuinely concerned about my welfare.

"Oh wow!" she gasped, shaking her head.

She suggested that I try the Salvation Army on Broad Street because it had a shelter. She went on to tell me, "If you tell them you are pregnant, they will help you find a place to live."

I said, "Thank you for the information," as I saw the bus approaching.

THE SEED OF THE CYCLE IS PLANTED

Monica stood looking at me for a second, and then said, "Hey, catch the bus with me and I'll take you there."

I hesitated at first, but then I thought, "What the hell?" It wasn't like I had any plans.

On the bus, Monica explained to me all about the shelter. She told me that the shelter partners with a program that provides help for single mothers who are pregnant. She reiterated that the shelter would take care of me and help me to find a place to live.

I was nervous getting off the bus and walking with a stranger, however, I did not know what to do and certainly did not have any other options. Besides, there was a faint sense of trust that made me follow her. As we approached the building, I moved a little closer to Monica because quite a few homeless people were waiting outside to speak with someone in the shelter.

I stood by the door, in the corner, as I watched Monica walk over to an older slender woman. The woman was wearing glasses. She had a caramel complexion framed with salt and pepper colored hair. She greeted Monica, and as they talked, they glanced over in my direction. When they were done talking, they headed towards me.

Monica said, "Margaret, this is Mrs. Harriett, and she runs this shelter. She's going to take good care of you and help you get on your feet." Monica mentioned something about the emancipation of a minor and said that Mrs. Harriett would explain it to me in more detail. She told me that the program would allow me to get a place to live for my baby and me. As I spoke with Mrs. Harriett, I could sense she was very concerned about my situation. When she paused our conversation, it gave me the opportunity to thank Monica for her help in accompanying me to the shelter. Deep down inside I wanted her to stay, and not leave me.

Eventually, Monica left, but she wished me well and gave me a hug. Mrs. Harriett asked me to come to her office with her. On the way in, I observed pictures and awards that she had received on display. I paused when I saw plaques with scriptures. I made a mental note to myself that she was a believer.

Once inside her office, she asked me to have a seat and tell her all about myself. I was lost for words. I began stumbling through my own mind looking for a way to tell her about myself. Obviously, she saw my dilemma and took charge of the conversation. To get the information she needed to help me, she asked questions. By the end of our conversation, she knew that my mom had kicked me out because I was pregnant.

When Mrs. Harriett asked about the father of my baby, I told her it was a student that didn't want a thing to do with me. She explained the rules for living in the shelter and estimated that

THE SEED OF THE CYCLE IS PLANTED

it would take about two weeks before locating a place for me to live. She also told me that she would be taking me to see an OB/GYN doctor to evaluate the baby and start me on prenatal vitamins.

When Mrs. Harriett finished explaining everything, I took a deep breath, hoping that everything she told me would come true. I must say, Mrs. Harriett was a nice woman. Two weeks after being in the shelter, Mrs. Harriett gave me the keys to my apartment and drove me to my new home. We turned into the Projects, and as her car came to a slow stop, I saw a sign that read, "Lake Olmstead."

I wouldn't say that my mom was rich, but we had lived in a good neighborhood. I stepped out of the car and looked around. I was definitely in an unfamiliar environment. There were kids running wild everywhere! I could hear loud music blasting from various apartments. Groups of people were on every other corner, just hanging out.

My mind was racing, but Mrs. Harriett interrupted my thoughts with another "take charge" conversation. We walked inside my apartment, and I froze in awe! Mrs. Harriett had gone to the thrift shop and furnished the apartment. She also put food in the refrigerator, gave me a WIC card to get me started, and said that I would be receiving a food stamp card in the mail.

I thanked Mrs. Harriett for everything that she had done for me. We embraced, and I held her for as long as I could. She reminded me of the grandmother I wished I had. As she was leaving, Mrs. Harriett said, "Don't forget about me. Stop by and see me from time to time. Stay in school, and if you want a job after school, there are plenty of restaurants hiring. Be sure to report any income to the housing and welfare office."

I told her that I heard everything she said and would take heed, and then we said our goodbyes. I locked the door behind Mrs. Harriett and took a tour of every room in my new apartment. I sat on the bed to take it all in. Just a few days ago, I was homeless. Today I had my own place. The outcome from such a traumatic experience had a far better ending than I could ever have imagined.

About a month after I decided to leave school, I heard a knock at the door. I slowly moved out of bed to peek through the blinds. I looked out and saw that it was Mrs. Harriett. I did not come to the door, so she got back into her car and drove away. I wondered if Mrs. Harriett knew that I had been out of school for a month. Or was she just stopping by to check on me? Was I afraid to face her knowing there's a possibility of her already knowing the truth?

As I was getting back in bed, I mumbled to myself, "Well, so much for making Mrs. Harriett proud of me. She asked me to do one thing, stay in school, and I couldn't even do that."

I really couldn't see my life getting any better. I was carrying a monster's baby. I looked down at my stomach and couldn't believe how big the baby was getting.

School was definitely not for me. I felt like I never belonged and being pregnant was just another reason not to go back. I was not about to give my classmates something else to talk about or the pleasure of humiliating me. I was good at hiding my stomach, but its growth had gotten beyond my control. I could no longer hide my pregnancy. "Farewell, Lucy Laney High School!"

7

BLACK (THE SNAKE): SAME SCRIPT—DIFFERENT CAST
Margaret

I believed my life was a bottomless pit. My life could not have gotten any worse. I finally gave birth to a baby girl, and I named her Renee. My next-door neighbor, Mrs. Cooper, watched Renee while I worked at Wendy's. I was doing the best I could, working to take care of a child that I didn't ask for.

How could I love someone who looked just like the person I feared? My daughter was the reason that I no longer felt hurt by Melvin, but she also reminded me of all the years of abuse. I didn't know how I was supposed to feel about this baby, or what to think. I had mixed emotions.

As soon as I felt like my life was manageable or somewhat under my control, Black came into the picture. Black was the neighborhood drug dealer who had been watching me since the day Mrs. Harriett brought me to the Projects. I remember seeing him when Mrs. Harriet pulled up to my apartment. When I got out of the car and looked across the street, my eyes immediately locked with him, and they would have stayed locked if it wasn't for Mrs. Harriet striking up a conversation with me.

Every time Black saw me, he took the opportunity to "spit his game." I guess you are wondering this: if I knew it was a game, why did I choose to play? The only answer I can think of is that he was persistent. His persistence had me second-guessing whether it was a game or not since I thought it didn't take long for a person to show their true colors.

You see, what I had to learn about a snake, is that it takes its time and moves slowly, responding differently to different people. So that's why it was hard to figure Black out, at first. After five months of shutting him down, I finally let my guard down just a little bit, and he slithered his way right on in.

Before I knew it, everything that was mine was his, including my life. He was a very cautious person, and that should have been an indicator to run. I knew he was twenty years old, which made him four years older than me. He told me that he was the Project supplier and that he didn't want this street job but had a rough life. He told me that he had no choice but to do it if he wanted to survive.

He served me all those words on a silver platter, and I ate them up. I will never forget the night I came downstairs watching him sniff this white powdery substance up his nose. At that moment, I should have gone back upstairs, but I was curious and wanted to know what it was. That was a mistake I will regret for the rest of my life.

Sniffing the powder for the first time was very uncomfortable. My nose hurt badly. The drugs sped up my heart. It felt like someone was pounding on my heart with a stick as the substance trickled down the back of my throat. I remember telling Black that this was not for me, but he convinced me to do it several times so that I could get used to it, to see if I would like it. All it took was a couple of times using, and I was hooked.

One day after getting high, I looked at the coffee table, and when I saw all the piles of empty bags on the table that Black and I had gone through, I was shocked that my body had not shut down. Black was loving the fact that he could bring another person down, so he introduced me to crack.

He had a great sales pitch! He told me that crack delivered the sensation faster, providing a stronger feeling and a bit more of that euphoria that I was looking for. I quickly grabbed the bag of rocks out of his hand and waited for instructions on how it's done. At that moment, I agreed to sell my soul to the devil and kill myself slowly. My life had changed significantly like a violent tornado, and it all started from a sniff of coke.

Since letting Black into my life, I now had two kids, and two baby daddies: one baby with Melvin, the monster; and one baby with Black, the devil. Black got into some trouble with the law and is now serving a life sentence for murder. I was twenty-two years old and a crackhead. Sadly, I was on my way to see Rodney, for my next fix.

8

REGGIE MACK JR.
His Story
Reggie

I looked out into an open field to watch a group of boys playing football. I chuckled when I saw a young boy raise both hands in the air as he screamed "Touchdown!"

Watching the boys play brought back so many memories. I often asked myself and God, "How did I go from being drafted by the Oakland Raiders to what society calls, a 'crackhead?'"

Wow! The memories of being a quarterback star flooded my thoughts. Growing up, I thought I would never make anything out of my life. My vision of myself changed when I realized that my athletic abilities could hold a bright future for me. In my senior year, I was the starting quarterback for Laney High School. Everywhere I went, people knew me by my performance on the field.

I remembered vividly what went down in the locker room before the team took the field. Some of the team would sit in a circle telling jokes, others would be listening to music, and there were some — including me — who would sit in silence, strategizing football plays in our minds.

I embraced all of my football experiences. Football gave me a sense of belonging. I no longer felt like an outcast. I had friends. As a matter of fact, my best friend Desmond was a running back on the team.

I can still hear Coach Jackson's baritone voice saying, "Alright, bring it in."

Upon hearing that command, the team surrounded Coach Jackson as he moved into the center. The coach was well respected, so he always had everyone's undivided attention. He was a father figure to the players. He always pushed us to do our best on and off the field. He pushed us to pursue our education too.

Before each game, he would say, "Alright, fellas, tonight we're going to show everyone who really runs the South. You know what we are going to say to them when we destroy them on the field?"

The team would then break out into a chant, "Na-na-na, na-na-na-na, hey, hey, hey, goodbye!"

Desmond and I led the team out of the locker room, walking side by side. Desmond would say, "Hey, Reggie, are you ready to dominate and destroy?"

"Hell yeah! I was born ready," I replied.

Once on the field, I stood on the sidelines with butterflies in the pit of my stomach, wearing my red jersey, number 8. I was the skinny kid with glasses and a big appetite, but never grew. Today, standing six-foot, five inches tall, 190 pounds and boasting a six-pack, I was what all the ladies wanted.

I remember looking out into the stands where men, women, and children filled the stadium. Some held signs with my name, some with my number, others chanted my name. I took it all in. I had fans, and I must admit, it felt good.

When the team heard the band crank up, that was our cue to stand behind the banner that read "Let's Go Wildcats!" It was held by a cheerleader on each side. As the band got louder, the team was psyched up. We jumped up and down and danced with the crowd. On cue from Coach Jackson, we burst through the banner, ready to dominate the game. While the team got into formation, Desmond and I walked to the center of the field to meet the referees and the opponents. I could look at my opponents and could tell that they had heard about me.

I was enjoying reminiscing about football until I was interrupted by my crack demon, which needed to be fed. I quickly pulled the phone from my pocket and dialed Rodney. He answered on the fourth ring.

"Hey, Rodney, are you still in the hood?" I asked.

Rodney said, "What's up, Reggie? I'm still here."

I told him that I was on my way to get a fix.

I cruised through traffic, eager to see Rodney so I could feed my demon. When I arrived at the location we were supposed to meet, I slowed down and parked on the opposite side of the street. I looked across the street and saw Rodney leaning against a burgundy box Chevy with tinted windows.

9

THE MEET AND GREET
Reggie

Rodney was a real cool guy. He was older than me, but not by much. He always treated me with respect, and never judged me because of my habit. I observed Rodney and his crew as I walked over, especially their style of clothing. They looked like triplets wearing white beaters and jeans.

"Wassup, Rodney! Dang, this is one nice summer," I shouted as I greeted him.

Turning my head to the right, I saw a fine sistah walking down the street in a nice summer dress. She had a caramel complexion. Her hair was pulled into a ponytail, and she was moving like she had somewhere to be. I was talking with Rodney, but soon he noticed that he no longer had my attention.

"Oh, that's Margaret," Rodney said.

"She's one of my regulars."

I just looked at him and smiled.

"She used to be built like a stallion, before she fell in love with crack," Rodney added.

I said, "Hell, she's still fine to me."

As Margaret headed toward us, I admired her beauty, but when she stood in front of me, I knew we possessed the same demon. Margaret stood with her arms folded, with an impatient look on her face.

"Hey, my name is Reggie," I blurted out.

She glanced at me for a second, but immediately her attention was back on Rodney.

"Rodney, I don't have all day. You already know what I need and want," yelled Margaret.

Rodney and Margaret made an exchange as I looked on.

Suddenly I yelled, "Dang, Rodney, you're rude as hell! Didn't you see me talking to Margaret?"

"Why are you speaking to me?" asked Margaret.

I looked over at Rodney who was trying hard not to laugh. After she got what she came for, Margaret was on her way. I just stood there and watched her walk away. She had hypnotized me, and for the past couple of years, only crack was able to do that.

"Margaret is as tough as nails," Rodney said.

"I see that," I replied.

I told Rodney that I would catch up with him later and left. I drove to my special location, an abandoned house on Perry Avenue, where I could feed my demon.

I remember walking up to the brick house with broken windows, graffiti all over the door, and pushing it open. I walked on stained carpet covered with old newspapers and used condoms. The awful stench of feces and urine from the toilet was overwhelming. I headed down a hallway that led to the last room on the right, hoping that there would be no one in there.

I'm not like others who like to have a crowd around them. I like to feed my demon in private. Opening the door, I was relieved to see that I had the room to myself. Nothing was in the room but one window with torn up blinds. I went over to the opposite side of the room from the window and slid down to the floor.

I took out my shooter, put my rocks in, and lit it. I began to hear the crackling sound from the crack being smoked. I thought to myself, "Hmm, that's probably how it got the name crack."

I leaned my head back against the wall and began to nod. Instead of going to sleep, I resumed reminiscing about my days as a high school football star. My mind went back to the homecoming game against the TW Josey Eagles. In that game, I threw the winning pass to Desmond and he caught it in the endzone. After the game, we walked out with the team, wearing letterman jackets. People were walking up to us saying, "Good job!" The girls tugged on our jackets. I walked tall and proud. You couldn't tell me nothin'.

As my crack high came down, I saw Margaret's face. It was as if she was standing right in front of me. I shook my head to clear my mind. I remember thinking, "Man, that sistah got to me. I want her bad!"

10

LET'S PLAY HOUSE
Margaret

"Mommy, I'm hungry," my oldest daughter whined. I woke up to her standing at the edge of the bed holding her teddy bear in one hand and sucking her thumb with the other hand.

"Give me a minute, Renee. Go play with your sister, and I'll get up in a minute and get you some cereal."

"Yay! Fruit Loops!" she screamed.

Renee took off running, all smiles, knowing she would get her favorite cereal. I turned over on my side admiring my man—my Reggie. Looking at him sleeping peacefully, a small smile crept up on my face. I loved waking up next to him. He was the best thing that had happened to me since sliced bread. I put my hands on his chest and whispered, "I love you," careful to not stir him out of his sleep.

Let me tell you about our love story. I remember the first time I met Reggie. It's crazy because we had the same demon in common—crack. And even though I loved him more than my children or myself, I never loved him more than crack and he was the same with me. Although we came from two different worlds, our addictions would forever bond us together.

The very first time we met, I was speed walking down the block, in a hurry to get a fix. It was mid-summer, and it was hot as hell. Sweat was dripping off my face and flowing all over my body. The sundress I had on was about two sizes too big, due to all the weight I had lost. Don't get it twisted: I used to be fine as hell. Standing five feet, seven inches tall, I had long curvaceous legs, a plump thick ass, and smooth dark skin. It was my looks that got me through the worst parts of my life. I had always depended on my looks to help me survive. My addiction had gotten the best of me, and I was surely letting myself go.

When I met up with my drug dealer, Rodney, I noticed a fine-looking man with him. That man was Reggie. For a moment, a millisecond, I was slightly embarrassed, but the embarrassment flew right out the window when it came to feeding my demon. That's the reason I was there. I wanted crack more than any fine-looking man. I had been in love with crack so long that I didn't realize that a man could awaken me, but this man did.

Reggie was tall, athletically built, with smooth golden-brown skin, and beautiful brown eyes. He was looking too good. He had me evaluating every inch of him that I could see. I remember thinking to myself, "Who is this dude? Could he be a new dope boy on the block?"

Reggie didn't look like a crackhead. However, I could be wrong, because I knew a lot of functional crackheads. Functional crackheads are those who work nine to five jobs, some with wives and children, who go about their daily lives not missing a step. But privately, they are crack addicts.

I was good at first just standing there admiring this man, but my demon was growing hungrier and woke me up from my fantasy. I was growing agitated. I had not smoked all day, and it was hot as hell. I rolled my eyes and crossed my arms against my chest, tapping my feet loudly on the ground, very impatiently waiting for Rodney. My crack demon was like a personal gnat that would not leave me alone. Finally, I cut Rodney off, mid-conversation and said, "You already know what I need." I handed him crumpled up bills.

"Well, hey to you too, Margaret," Rodney responded, as he went into his stash to break me off some.

Reggie said, "Dang! You're rude as hell. You don't see me and my boy chopping it up? Trying to handle business?"

I didn't care who he was. No one stands in my way of getting high. This fine man just stood staring at me. It frustrated me to see him staring, so I yelled, "What the hell are you looking at?"

I cannot stand for people to stare at me. He told me to calm down and asked for my name, but I ignored him. Even though he was fine, my crack demon ran my life, and it was telling me to get home so that I could feed him. I guess you could say crack was my man because I got my crack and headed home.

Eventually, Reggie and I met again. We actually hung out at the same place that was safe for smokers, homeless people, shooters, or whoever wanted to be there. All I wanted to do was get high and be at peace.

There was a lot of tension between Reggie and me when we met. He asked me why I was so rude earlier. I explained to him that I wanted to get high, and the conversation blossomed from there. We stayed up all night smoking. Turns out, he used to be a very well-known football player in high school and college. He injured

LET'S PLAY HOUSE

his knee, and that resulted in him losing an NFL draft spot with the Oakland Raiders.

11

WEB OF DECEIT
Margaret

Crack was the bond that formed my relationship with Reggie. I was aware that I was jacked up. My intentions were never to love him, but to get all I could out of him. People can call me what they want to call me, but I learned at an early age that this was a cruel, cold world and that not even parents give a damn about you.

I was trying to drown the painful memories of my mother who allowed my stepdad to walk into my room and take what he wanted while she looked the other way. Then she had the nerve to call me everything but a child of God when her husband got me pregnant. She kicked me out on the streets to fend for myself and a child I didn't want or ask for.

Life has been cruel, so I couldn't care less about anyone else. I felt that way until I met

Reggie. I became a little soft around the edges when I met him. I always thought that I was not capable of loving someone. My love for Reggie and my love for crack became a tug of war. Sad to say, crack was winning.

I was so lost on memory lane that it took a moment for me to realize that my name was being called.

Reggie was shouting, "Margaret! are you okay?"

"Yes, I'm fine," I said.

Reggie said that he had been calling my name for a minute. I assured him that I was not ignoring him but had just gotten lost in my thoughts. Reggie got out of bed and got ready for work. I didn't want to move. For days I had been tired and my breast hurt. I wanted my cycle to hurry up and come because I was tired of feeling this way. I took a deep breath and got up to fix the kids some cereal.

On the way up, I felt the urge to vomit, so I ran to the bathroom. I made it just in time to throw up over the toilet. I slid down to the floor because I felt awful. When I looked up, Reggie was standing in the doorway with a concerned look on his face.

He asked, "Babe, what's wrong?"

I replied, "I'm okay. It's probably something I ate last night. I must stop eating so late at night."

Reggie asked, "Do you want me to stay home with you?"

"No babe. I'll be fine. Go ahead and get to work," I replied.

I waited for him to walk downstairs before I decided to get up from the floor. I stood up, washed my face, brushed my teeth, and headed downstairs. When I got to the kitchen, the girls were in the corner of the kitchen playing with a tea set. As I was about to open the refrigerator to get milk, I froze. The calendar on the refrigerator made me realize that we were three days into a new month. I fixed cereal for the kids and went to sit on the couch to calm myself down. All of the symptoms I was experiencing suggested I might be pregnant again. Reggie and I didn't want to have kids. Honestly, I was not even sure that the baby was Reggie's.

I love drugs so much that I was greedy for them. I would have my own drugs and money, but I would still sell my body for more drugs without hesitation. Greed had screwed me up big time. You can say that if I loved Reggie, I wouldn't have slept with other men. But, when it comes to this crack demon, I have no soul, mind, or heart. The only thing I care about is feeding the demon that feeds me.

I laid around all day thinking of what I should do. The first thing I needed to do was confirm that I was pregnant and go from there.

I heard the screen door open and it alarmed me. I didn't realize that it was time for Reggie to come home.

When Reggie saw me, he asked, "Are you feeling better?"

I said, "Yeah, I'm feeling a little better."

"Do you want me to go get some candy from Rodney?" asked Reggie.

"Yes," I replied.

We used the word 'candy' instead of crack when the kids were in the room. While Reggie went to get some candy, I sat gawking at the TV as I waited impatiently for him to return. My nerves were a wreck. I had to find out if I was pregnant. My plan was to get a pregnancy test kit as soon as Reggie got back.

Soon, Reggie returned home. He was excited that Rodney had given him enough drugs for both of us to get high. Now that Reggie was back, I knew that he would be determined to figure out what was bothering me. He loved me so much. He would do anything to make me smile. As he entered the living room, he saw me gazing at the wall. I didn't even see him watching me.

As I sat in silence, Reggie said, "Hey babe! I'm back."

I didn't say anything to him, but I got up and walked past him as if I was sleepwalking, and went into the bedroom.

Reggie shouted, "Babe! Where are you going? I've got your antidote."

I turned and looked at him holding a bag of crack in his hand hoping to lure me towards him. Instead, I went into the bedroom to come up with a game plan. I had to get a pregnancy test done without Reggie finding out what I was doing. After sitting for a while, I got up and peeped out of the bedroom door and saw him sitting on the couch looking at the bag of crack in his hand.

He had a look of confusion on his face as he glided his hands repeatedly over his head and face in frustration. He shook his head a couple of times as if he was trying to reset his mind. He leaned back on the couch with his eyes focused on the ceiling. After a few minutes, it appeared that he was in deep thought.

∼

12

FLAG ON THE PLAY
Reggie

As I lay holding the bag of crack, gazing at the ceiling in frustration, I began to ask myself, "Why am I an addict? How did I get to this place?" As I reviewed the timeline of my addiction roadmap in my mind, I dropped the bag of crack to the floor.

At first thought, the answer to me was obvious, "I'm weak! Maybe that's what my father saw in me ever since I was a child."

To put it all out there, my father, Reggie Mack Sr., was the biggest drug dealer in the east boundary area. He moved crack cocaine from the West to the Southeast. He was nobody to play with. He put fear in everyone—including me.

My father was in the streets, but I never knew about it. Perhaps my father believed that I should already know about the streets, as if it was supposed to come naturally for me.

I was a skinny kid with glasses and a large appetite, but I never grew. I was book smart, but street dumb. All of my life, I tried to make my father proud of me. It looks as if I have failed to accomplish this.

When I failed at things, I could always see the disappointment in my dad's eyes. On the other hand, my mother always comforted me and told me that I would do better the next time. Numerous times, I would overhear my parents discussing me, and Mom would constantly say, "Why don't you spend any time with your son? You are treating him as if he is not yours." Dad never gave her an explanation, just that he was busy and left it at that.

The only time I thought my father may have been proud of me was when I joined the football team in high school. I remember the day that football built a bond between my father and me. I was never going to tell him I had joined the football team.

I decided to get involved in football because I needed to do something besides stay in the house. Also, I remembered Mom telling me how she first met my dad at Lucy Craft Laney High School. Mom was a cheerleader and Dad a football player. According to Mom, Dad was a damn good football player. Unfortunately, he blew his knee out and did not get the chance to play college football.

FLAG ON THE PLAY

I remember the day when my coach called me into his office and told me that I was the only freshman starting on the varsity team. My position was the quarterback — the same position my dad played in high school. I beamed with excitement as I ran home.

I burst through the front door, yelling, "Mom! Mom!"

Mom came running out of the kitchen shouting, "What junior? What's going on?"

She motioned for me to calm down. As I was trying to calm down, I saw Dad lying back in his recliner with his feet propped up looking at sports news.

I told mom, "Coach Jackson told me that I am going to be a quarterback! He also told me that I will be the only freshman starting on the varsity team."

Mom said, "Junior, that is good news. I'm so proud of you!" She grabbed me and gave me a big long hug.

My Dad asked, "What's all the noise about?"

I hung my head down because I didn't know how to talk to him. I was always afraid that I was going to do or say the wrong thing to him.

Mom spoke for me as she always did. She said, "I told you months ago that Junior was trying out for football. Don't you remember?"

Dad said, "Oh, yeah. It must have slipped my mind," as he sat looking at me.

Mom broke his stare and said, "You were a star quarterback, right?"

Dad yelled, "Hell yeah! I was one of the best Lucy Craft Laney High School had, in my day!" as he lit up like a light bulb.

Dad was suddenly so proud of me that he asked me to get a football and show him what I've got. I grabbed my football from my room, and as I was coming back to the living room, Dad was already waiting for me at the front door. Mom beamed with excitement, holding her hands together in a praying position. I remember thinking to myself, *"God has answered my prayer and Mom's prayer."*

I followed Dad out the door and across the street to the open field. Throwing balls with him was exhilarating. I gave my ball a perfect spin as it sailed through the air to my dad. I smiled at the shocked look on his face as he saw me throw the ball at the speed of a rocket. This time spent with my dad finally let me know that I had found something that I was good at and that it made my dad very proud of me.

Football allowed me to bond with my father. I wanted my father to be proud of his son and glad that he had created me. My dad attended my games.

I will never forget the first time I threw a touchdown pass, and the announcer said, "Number 8—Quarterback Reggie Mack Jr. —TOUCHDOWN!"

Everyone was on their feet calling out my name, but the one person that mattered the most was my father. I looked at my father and saw him up on his feet yelling, "That's my son! Come on, Junior! Let's get another one!"

I stood, thinking, "*I want to play football for the rest of my life, just to keep my dad happy and proud.*"

My high school years went by like a breeze. In my senior year, I was awarded the Heisman Trophy, and colleges came from all over to recruit me for their team. Dad and I were particularly close during the NFL draft season. I was ecstatic that I had a chance to be drafted. My dad stood right by my side. Mom was no longer my spokesperson. Dad had that honor. In the end, I chose Georgia Tech in Atlanta, Georgia, which was about two and a half hours from home.

I enjoyed coming home on the weekends so my dad and I could enjoy our favorite holiday — Football Sunday. Mom would be in the kitchen cooking Sunday dinner while Dad and I were in the living room watching the game. As we watched the games, Dad took the time to explain different plays and give me advice on how to become a better player. Those were the best times of my life. My dad and I were inseparable.

13

ALMOST DOESN'T COUNT
Reggie

With the bag of crack still lying on the floor, a flood of emotions overwhelmed me. I recalled the painful interruption in my life when my football career came to an unforeseen end.

It was supposed to be my last college game before I went off to summer camp with the Oakland Raiders. I tore my anterior cruciate ligament (ACL). In preparation to throw the ball to a receiver, my right hand was a little past my shoulder when I got hit from both sides, resulting in my knee twisting. I tried to get up from the hit, but severe pain caused me to fall back down to the ground.

I didn't get up again.

I was grabbing my right knee above the knee cap when I heard Coach yell, "Stay down!"

The medic team and my teammates ran toward me and surrounded me. I closed my eyes as tears flooded down my face. The tears kept flowing as I was lifted onto a gurney and carried off the field. I kept my eyes closed. I did not want to look at anyone, including my father.

Shortly after arriving at the hospital, the doctor confirmed that I had torn my ACL. I watched as Coach Roger and my dad walked out of the room with the doctor to discuss my diagnosis. They made me feel like a five-year-old by excluding me from the conversation. It wasn't long before Coach Roger returned to the room with Dad, who stood in the doorway.

Coach Roger said, "Son, I really hate to be the bearer of bad news. Unfortunately, the doctor is not sure when you will be able to play football again. The Oakland Raiders will not wait for you to recover from your injury. They have made the decision to choose another player to join their roster."

The room was quiet. Every eye was on me as if I was a corpse in a casket at my funeral.

I tried to be a man like my father wanted me to be and not cry, however, the boy inside of me won the battle. My head fell back on my pillow as tears cascaded from my eyes.

Mom came to my bedside to comfort me, but there was nothing anyone could say or do. That day, I cried myself to sleep.

When I woke up, my dad was standing at the window with both hands in his pockets.

I said, "Dad, I am so sorry. I never meant for this to happen."

He wasted no time in coming close to me.

He said, "The Macks have been having bad luck for generations. It appears ain't nothing is going to change. You made it further than I did, but you didn't make it to the finish line."

I watched my dad turn and walk out of my hospital room. My heart was hurting. I wanted to die.

Margaret suddenly emerged from the bedroom. She interrupted my trip down memory lane.

Margaret asked, "Can I have my drugs?"

I gave her the drugs and she quickly went back into the bedroom, slamming the door behind her. I sat there shaking my head not knowing what to do. Margaret was the first woman that I had ever loved. I decided to give her some space, because I didn't want to add to what was causing her to be upset.

14

THE DREAM THAT DIED
Reggie

Since it was clear that Margaret wanted to be alone, I pulled out my shooter and began to smoke. As I smoked, I resumed analyzing how my life went off track and how I ended up being a crack addict.

After my hopes for the NFL draft ended, I stayed in college. I majored in architecture, and after college, I went to work for my dad as a head foreman. Surprisingly, Dad gave up the street life and started his own construction company.

Working for Dad in a construction company wasn't where I wanted to work, but it was a job. Every morning, I dreaded going to work. I was miserable, and it showed. I should have been happy with what I had, but working at a construction company was not in my plans.

One day, at work, all of the guys were talking trash about who was going to win the game.

THE LINEAGE: BREAKING THE CYCLE

Everyone was excited and couldn't wait to celebrate Super Bowl Sunday. As luck would have it, the Oakland Raiders made it to Super Bowl XV in 1981. They were joining the Philadelphia Eagles on the big stage. To see the Oakland Raiders in the big game was painful. If it had not been for my injury, there was a good chance I could have been with the Oakland Raiders enjoying the bliss of playing in Super Bowl XV.

Missing out on a huge opportunity to, possibly, be the starting quarterback for the Oakland Raiders' big game, was overwhelming. The more I thought about what woulda, coulda, shoulda happened, I became angry as hell.

While the guys were talking smack about the big game, my mind was a million miles away, thinking about how my life might be different today. I wasn't joining in the conversation, so Jared, one of my co-workers, asked, "Do you have any plans for the super bowl game?"

I said, "Naw, man, just gonna go home and chill."

Jared said, "Man, what type of life is that? It's not good to be home alone all the time. Do you like football?"

I paused for a moment before I answered because I was trying to determine my true answer. After a long pause, I said, "Yeah Jared, I like football."

He said, "Cool! That means you can come to my boy's home for a Super Bowl party." He scribbled the address for the party on a piece of paper and handed it to me.

On my way home from work, I thought about Jared's statement that it's not good to be in the house all the time. I didn't want to admit it. He was right. I spent a lot of time alone. I had friends, or at least I thought I had friends. Truth be told: I didn't have any friends. I used to believe that Desmond was my best friend but learned differently after I got injured playing football. Desmond didn't come to the hospital to see me, nor did he return my calls. He was only my friend when he saw me as a winner, someone that he could be attached with.

It was two days before Super Bowl XV, and I didn't want to attend any parties. I failed to come up with a good excuse to tell the guys on Monday why I didn't show for the party, so I went.

Walking up to the large brick house, cars were parked all the way down the street. When I heard someone call my name, I turned to see who it was, and it was Jared with a group of guys from work. Once inside the house, Jared introduced all of us to his friend Phil, who welcomed us and gave us a tour of the area of the house that the party would take place. After the tour, I headed to the kitchen for food and drinks.

Right before the game, I had to make a pit stop. It was hard to determine which closed door was the bathroom. I opened the door to what I thought was the bathroom, but it was the wrong room. When I opened the door, a group of guys were in a circle, passing around a pipe. Before I could close the door, one guy blurted out, "This will take away your pain." I didn't want to turn down a good smoke, so I indulged. Sadly, I was dumb enough to believe it was only a temporary fix. Before that smoke, I didn't know that I would have to keep smoking to ease my pain.

After taking a couple of smokes from the pipe, someone told me what I was smoking, and I went off on everyone. What I didn't admit to myself at the time was that I liked the feeling that it gave me. After my outburst, I stayed. I thought to myself that it was only a one-time thing, and I should be okay. Unfortunately, days later, I wanted to feel that sensation again.

I jumped up when I heard the kids crying. My trip down memory lane came to an abrupt end when the kids interrupted me. I put the pipe into my pocket and headed to the kitchen. The kids were crying because they were hungry. I comforted them and prepared them something to eat. After I fed the kids, I gave them baths and put them to bed.

The parenting chores made me wonder if I would ever father children of my own someday. With the kids comfortably in bed, it was time to comfort Margaret. She had spent too much time isolated in her own world.

∼

15

SOMETHING TO LIVE FOR
Margaret

Reggie knocked on the bedroom door until I was forced to open it. Slowly, I opened the door, but I didn't say a word. I climbed back into bed and turned my back toward him. He crawled into bed and wrapped his arm around me. Soon, we were asleep.

The next morning my mission was to get to the drugstore. I got things in order at home and headed to the pharmacy. Once in the store, I headed straight to the family planning aisle. I grabbed a pregnancy test and rushed to the bathroom. I watched in panic as the plus sign quickly appeared on the test screen. Dropping the test on the floor, I stood in disbelief at the results lying there. Tears running down my face, I was totally shocked.

I wiped my face as I looked in the mirror and said, "This secret, I must carry to my grave.

Reggie can never find out that there is a possibility that he could be a father."

On the way back home, my thoughts were scattered like a jigsaw puzzle. *"What am I supposed to do?"* This question played over and over in my mind like a broke record. As I approached the apartment, I could see Reggie through the window, sitting on the couch. I took a deep breath and opened the door.

I looked at Reggie, held out my hand, but didn't say one thing. He knew what I wanted. He gave me some crack, and I headed to the bedroom and locked the door. I didn't want any company. I hated being mean to Reggie, but that was the only way to get away from him without having to answer questions or engage in a conversation. I was sitting on the floor for about thirty minutes smoking when I recalled a conversation Reggie and I had some time ago. In that conversation, both of us said that we didn't want any kids together. This recollection made me wonder if he would give me some money to get rid of the baby if I would tell him I was pregnant. *"Wow! This might actually work!"* With this plan in mind, I decided to go to bed and talk with Reggie tomorrow.

Unexpectedly, a knock on the door woke me from my sleep. I forgot to unlock the door before I went to bed. Slowly, I dragged myself out of bed to unlock the door for Reggie.

I was hoping he would get in bed and go to sleep without wanting to talk. When he got in bed, he wrapped his arms around me and whispered in my ear, "Baby, we need to talk."

I said, "Not now. I'm tired."

He said, "I understand, but you've been pushing me away for days. So the sooner you tell me what's wrong, the sooner you can go back to sleep."

I took a deep breath and then turned to face him and said, "I'm pregnant."

Reggie stared at me as if he didn't hear a word I said.

I asked him, "Did you hear me? I'm pregnant."

Again, no response from Reggie.

After a stretch of silence, he cleared his throat and said, "I heard you."

Before he could say anything else, I said, "We've already had this conversation, and we are on the same page about not having a child together."

I asked, "Do you want me to get rid of the baby?"

Reggie appeared to be choked up, which was not a response I was expecting.

He said, "No. Wait a minute, Margaret."

He paused and then said, "Do you plan to be with me for the rest of your life?"

I was getting upset but trying hard not to show it.

"Yes," I said.

Reggie went on to say, "There is nothing wrong with us having someone we both created."

At this point, I was silent.

To my surprise, he went on and on about needing to change our lives, get off drugs, and focus on providing a better life for our children.

That was not what I wanted to do. I didn't want to change. I was fine with the life I was living. I had nothing to say.

I stared at him as he lay looking at the ceiling. I knew that look too well. He was getting lost in his own thoughts. I turned over on my side with my back facing him. At that moment, I only wanted to go to sleep.

I drifted off to sleep, but Reggie was too fired up to sleep. A flood of emotions overtook him. One minute, he was excited about being a father, and the next minute, he was sad. His emotions went from being happy to being scared in an unceasing cycle. He spent hours awake evaluating fatherhood.

Reggie became mentally exhausted from the news about being a father. He recalled the conversation they had about not having any children, but he also realized that saying what you will do in a particular situation is altogether different than when you find yourself facing that situation.

Reggie was acutely aware of his relationship with his father and often told himself that if he ever became a father, he was going to be a better dad than his father had been to him. With a baby on the way, Reggie believed that he had a chance to fulfill that promise.

He thought intensely about how he needed to change his drug addiction. The night was passing quickly, and he needed to rest. He closed his eyes and prayed, "God, please help me! I want to change my life for my child. I have something to live for."

∼

16

When Hope Failed

Reggie and Margaret decided to become parents. The nine months were not easy but they made it through. On March 22, 1987, Margaret gave birth to a beautiful baby girl, who they named, Reign Monroe Johnson. It was a happy occasion, and all of the family was present.

On the third day after giving birth, Margaret was up and moving around. She was delighted that the nurse told her that she could shower. Reggie graciously helped her to the bathroom to shower.

While Margaret was showering, Reggie's mom decided to go to the cafeteria to get something to eat. Reggie Sr. stayed with the baby while everyone was busy.

While holding the baby, a nurse came into the room and asked Reggie Sr., "Do you want a DNA test?"

"Yes," replied Reggie Sr.

The nurse told Reggie Sr. that a nurse would be coming shortly to get the baby for a bath. When the nurse arrived to bathe Reign, Reggie Sr. went to the cafeteria to see why his wife was taking a long time to return to the room.

After assisting Margaret with her shower, Reggie Jr. stepped out of the bathroom so Margaret could get dressed. Soon, a nurse came into the room and told Reggie that she was here to collect blood from the father of baby Reign. Reggie Jr. didn't even question the nurse. He freely gave her his arm to take the blood.

It was his first child, his first time as a dad, so he thought a blood test was routine for fathers. Four days after giving birth, Margaret and the baby were released to go home. Everyone was happy and excited.

As Margaret and Reggie were preparing to leave the hospital, a nurse walked into the room and handed Reggie Jr. a piece of paper. Reggie slowly lifted his head up from reading the paper. His face had a look of astonishment and shock. It looked as if he had seen a ghost.

Abruptly, uncontrollable tears began streaming down Reggie's face. His heart was pumping so hard that he thought perhaps he was having a heart attack!

Reggie asked himself, "What am I reading?"

In a rage of anger, he shouted from the top of his lungs, "Reign is not mine!"

Reggie laid Reign down in her baby basket. Margaret didn't know what to say to Reggie. She moved toward him in an attempt to comfort him, but he yelled, "Bitch, stay away from me! You don't care about anyone but yourself."

Reggie shoved Margaret away from him, glanced at Reign for one last time, and ran out of the hospital room.

Margaret was devastated. She crawled back into the hospital bed, buried her face in the pillow, and cried. She was completely heartbroken. At that moment, it became crystal clear to Margaret that she had lost the only person who ever loved her.

17

THE PAIN OF FATHERHOOD
Margaret

Simply put, I was horrified that Reggie had found out that he was not a father. Over the past nine months, there had been countless conversations in which Reggie poured out his heart to me about the joys of becoming a father. Coupled with the visible strides that he made to change his life, I knew that he was devastated. I am deeply aware that I caused his pain.

I am sure Reggie was asking himself, "Why can't I find someone who truly loves me? I am a good person. Why did Margaret do this to me?"

Reggie would never intentionally cause anyone pain, and he expected the same from others. Me, on the other hand — I'm selfish, and it's all about me most of the time. Reggie dealt with people mistreating him simply by moving on, but this betrayal cut him deep. I'm sure it hurt like hell.

I wasn't sure if Reggie could take any more pain or new setbacks in his life. He loved me so much. It would be difficult for him to come to grips with why I did this to him. He had changed so much for me and the baby. He wanted a new life with me, my kids, and our baby. He was ready. Crack had always been Reggie's prescription for pain and after today's events, I knew he would need some "candy" to ease his pain.

Margaret was right. Reggie called Rodney to let him know he was on the way to see him. On his way to Rodney, Reggie stopped at an ATM to get some extra cash. He was going to need more than his usual supply of crack.

Reggie met Rodney to get what he wanted. There was no talking. The transaction took place, and Reggie took off to his favorite crack house to ease his pains.

Reggie maneuvered through people scattered about in the crack house to find an empty, isolated room. Settled into his VIP section of the house, he began smoking to drown out his sorrows. The relentless flash of the DNA report loomed largely in his mind.

Thoughts of what Margaret had done were impossible to erase. Soon, Reggie had run out of crack and went out to meet Rodney again for more. He was relentless in trying to easing his pain. He was determined not to stop drugging until the pain subsided.

After purchasing a new batch of drugs, Reggie went back to his VIP room at the crack house. His heart was still focused on Margaret. He thought about the good times they had shared. Every time a bad memory came to mind, he smoked more crack to keep it from surfacing. Along with his memories of Margaret, memories of his football failure that disappointed his father also flooded his mind.

The DNA test was the final blow. The pain was unremitting and maintained a grip on Reggie's heart and mind. As the night progressed, Reggie's body began to signal that he needed to stop the drugs. As he tried to stand up to shake it off, his body went limp. He became light-headed and fell to the floor. He began to vomit uncontrollably and broke out in a cold sweat.

Reggie could not catch his breath, and soon, he could not move his body. He opened his mouth and tried with every fiber in his being to call for help, but no words came out. The pain was excruciating. He gasped for air as visions of his life flashed before his eyes. This would be the end.

Reggie resigned to stop fighting death and welcomed it, in hopes that things would be better on the other side. He closed his eyes and an image of his father appeared in his mind. He whispered, "Dad, I'm so sorry." He took his last breath.

18

HEY, DEATH, COME AND GET ME
Margaret

Two days after coming home from the hospital, there was a knock at my door. I was surprised to look out and see Rodney. I wondered why he came to my home. As I opened the door, I saw a grim look on his face.

Softly, Rodney said, "Reggie overdosed at the crack house."

I screamed, "No! No no, no, no," and slid down to the floor.

I laid on the floor crying in a fetal position.

It was only at that moment that I realized how much I truly loved Reggie, but it was too late.

Reggie's parents blamed me for his death, but that didn't bother me one bit, because I blamed me too. The family banned me from the funeral, but I sneaked in to see him before the family arrived for the wake.

At the wake, I hid in a corner and watched his father angrily yell, "God! I guess this is payback for all the lives I destroyed! Did you have to punish me by taking my only son?"

His father bent over the casket and cried bitterly. Reggie had always felt his father didn't love him, but by the looks of things, he did.

After Reggie's death, I had nothing to lose. I gave Reign up. I needed someone to blame, so I blamed my daughter. After I gave up Reign, my other two kids were taken from me.

It should be no surprise, that I am back in the crack house. Sitting on the floor smoking crack, I am hoping it will have mercy on me and completely numb my pains.

I have been in pain all of my life.

I begged God, "Let me die. I don't want to live anymore."

I didn't want to feel any more pain and the only option to escape it is death.

I began to rock back and forth as I listened to the crackling sounds of the pipe.

I resolved within myself to sit here and smoke crack, while I wait for death to come for me.

∽

Epilogue

The Lineage: Breaking the Cycle is the first in a series of three books.

As Margaret sat on the floor with tears streaming down her face, waiting for death to take her out of her misery, her hopes were shattered. Her excessive drugging did not hasten death to her door. Unfortunately, death was a no show. Death didn't have her number.

Margaret made it through that night, and for years, she continued living in a generational cycle of sexual, emotional, and psychological abuse that she did not choose to break. The cycle was passed to Margaret's children.

Will the cycle be broken?

Follow the stories of Margaret's children to learn if they will choose to accept or reject the cycle.

P.O. Box 453
Powder Springs, Georgia 30127
770.727.6517

info@entegritypublishing.com
www.entegritypublishing.com

www.ingramcontent.com/pod-product-compliance
Lightning Source LLC
Chambersburg PA
CBHW071023080526
44587CB00015B/2465